ROCK
SPELL -A- STORY

by Sharon Golub

C O N T E N T S

Design: Brendan Walsh

© 1994 WARNER BROS. PUBLICATIONS INC.
All Rights Reserved

Any duplication, adaptation or arrangement of the compositions
contained in this collection requires the written consent of the Publisher.
No part of this book may be photocopied or reproduced in any way without permission.
Unauthorized uses are an infringement of the U.S. Copyright Act and are punishable by Law.

THE BYRDS

what he h - [♪] -rd so much that he [♪] -ve them his song

Mr. Tambourine Man to r - [♪] -ord. It app- [♪] -r- [♪]

on their 1965 [♪] -ut album The Byrds and [♪] -me [♪]

num - [♪] - r one song. This r - [♪] -ord has [♪] - n

[♪] - ll - [♪] one of the all - time rock gr - [♪] - ts.

Turn , Turn , Turn , from their s - [♪] - ond album was

[♪] -tually [♪] pass- [♪] from the [♪] -ible that was set

to music. It pro- [♪] to [♪] -come [♪] million

seller. Other hits of theirs inclu - [♪] [♪] - ight Miles High,

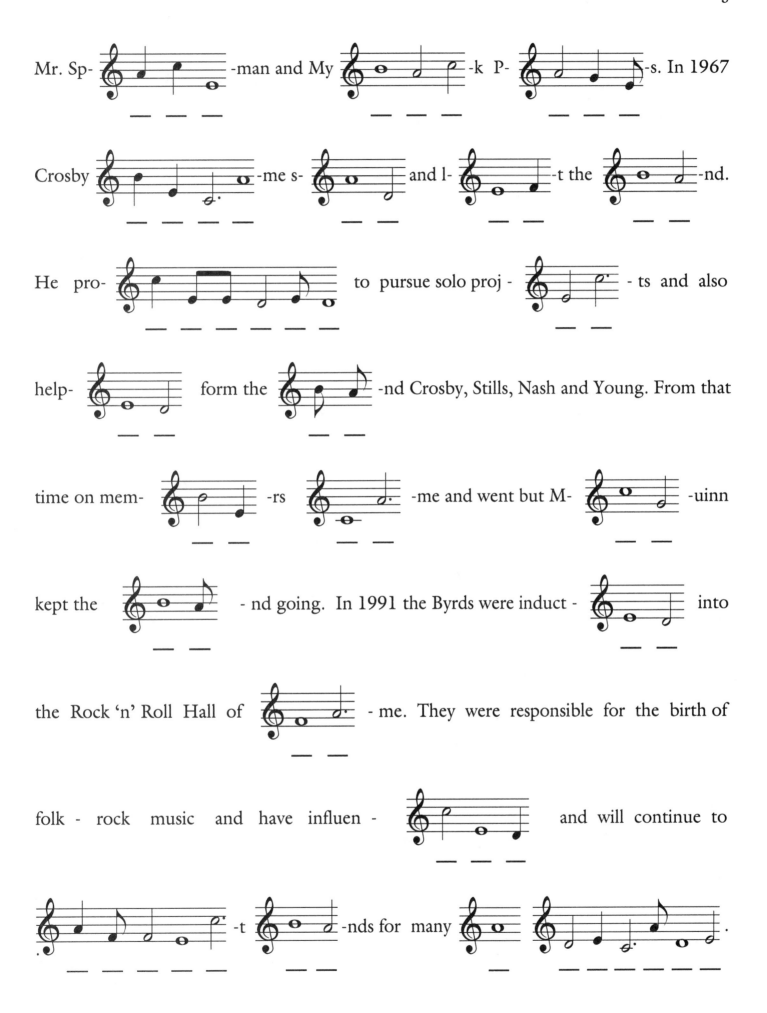

Mr. Sp- [music] -man and My [music] -k P- [music] -s. In 1967

Crosby [music] -me s- [music] and l- [music] -t the [music] -nd.

He pro- [music] to pursue solo proj - [music] - ts and also

help- [music] form the [music] -nd Crosby, Stills, Nash and Young. From that

time on mem- [music] -rs [music] -me and went but M- [music] -uinn

kept the [music] - nd going. In 1991 the Byrds were induct - [music] into

the Rock 'n' Roll Hall of [music] - me. They were responsible for the birth of

folk - rock music and have influen - [music] and will continue to

[music] -t [music] -nds for many [music] [music] .

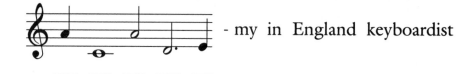

GENESIS

In 1966 at the Charterhouse - my in England keyboardist

Tony  -nks and singer Peter  -riel join-

with Anthony Phillips and Mike Rutherford to r -  - ord

 - mo tape. They sent it to  r -  - ord

produ - 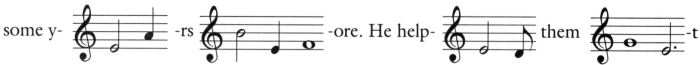 - r who h - atten - their school

some y-  -rs  -ore. He help- them  -t

 - l on R - - ords

and nam- 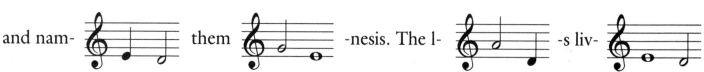 them -nesis. The l-  -s liv-

8

M - ♪ - hanics h - ♪ much su - ♪ - ss with hits such as All I N - ♪ Is ♪ Mir- ♪ -le. Collins also ♪ -i- ♪ ♪ solo album ♪ -ll- ♪ ♪ Value. The ♪ - nd stay - ♪ to - ♪ - ther and in 1981 the ♪ -nesis album ♪ was another gr- ♪ -t su - ♪ - ss. Their song Tonight, Tonight, Tonight was ♪ major su - ♪ - ss and was also the music to ♪ TV ♪ - r commercial. Collins never ♪ - ndon - ♪ ♪ - nesis and ♪ - spite the many mem- ♪ -r chan- ♪ -s they man - ♪ to stay one of the ♪ - st ♪ - nds

in rock into the 1990's.

CROSBY, STILLS, NASH & YOUNG

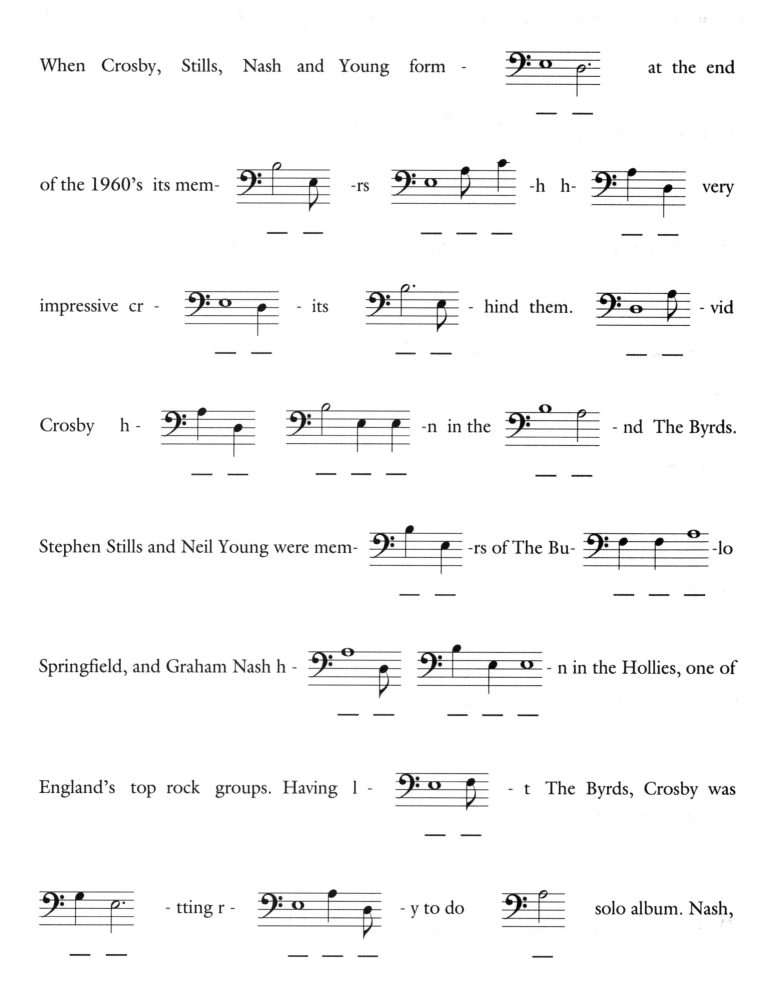

still with the Hollies was visiting him, and Stills was trying to ♪ -i- ♪

what to do next with his ♪ -r- ♪ -r. Fooling around in the living

room, they start - ♪ singing and playing to - ♪ - ther. They

lov- ♪ what they h- ♪ -rd, took their ♪

and h- ♪ for England in 1968 to write and reh- ♪ -rse.

Crosby and Nash were responsible for the ♪ -nd's an- ♪ -l-like

harmonies, not too ♪ and not too ♪ ,

and Stills wrote their finest songs. Their ♪ - ut album was one of the

♪ -st in folk-rock history. Neil Young ♪ -me ♪ -oard

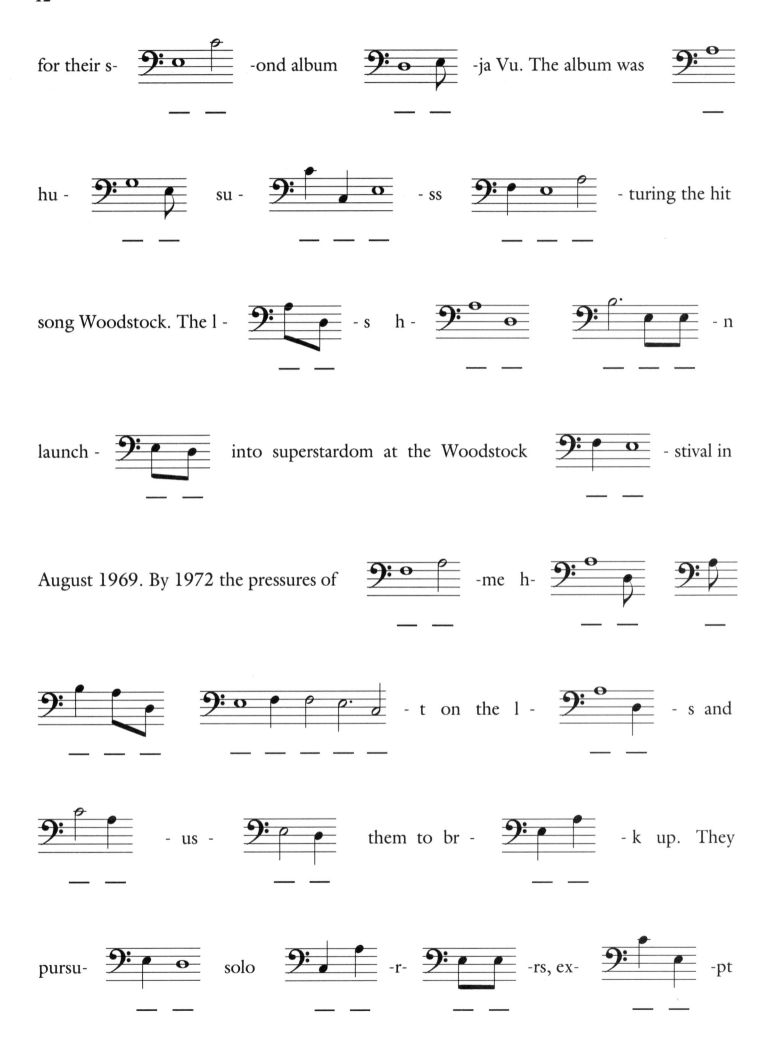

12

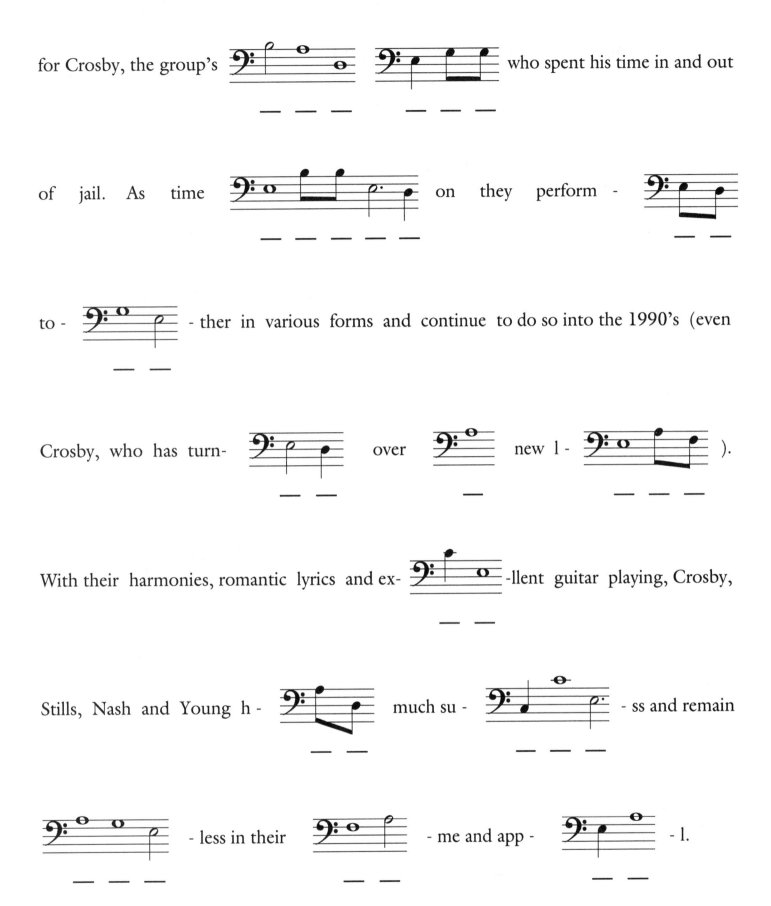

for Crosby, the group's who spent his time in and out

of jail. As time on they perform -

to - ther in various forms and continue to do so into the 1990's (even

Crosby, who has turn- over new l -).

With their harmonies, romantic lyrics and ex- -llent guitar playing, Crosby,

Stills, Nash and Young h - much su - - ss and remain

- less in their - me and app - - l.

YES

In [♪♪♪♪] -m- [𝅝] -r 1968 [𝅝] -ter

returning to his home in England from [♩] [𝅝] -i- [♪] in

[♩.] -rmany, sin- [♪♪] -r Jon An- [♪𝅝] -rson met

[♩.] -ss player Chris Squire. To- [♩𝅝] -ther, they form- [♪♪]

the foun- [𝅝♩] -tion of Yes, one of the l- [♪♪♪] -ing rock 'n' roll

[𝅝♩.] -nds of the 1970's. They were unique in that they were not

[♪♪] -raid to [♪♩] innovators and they got their inspiration from all

kinds of music, classi- [♩♩] -l to rock. The [♪♪] -nd's first two albums did not [♪] - in much attention and neither did they until some

y - [♪] - rs later. They m - [♪] some mem - [♪] - r

chan- [♪] - s and the [♪] -nd's style [♪] - n

to improve. An - [♪] - rson's songwriting was [♪] - tting

[♪] - tter and their music as [♪] whole was starting to blend. Their

third album was quite [♪] su - [♪] - ss. [♪] - ore

their [♪] - ut Unit - [♪] States tour, they

m - [♪] another chan - [♪] and keyboard virtuoso Rick

Wakeman was [♪] . Yes's style was to play lon- [♪] -r

16

pi - [♪] - s of music, with exciting visual st - [♪] shows.

Sometimes one song would last twenty minutes. Roun - [♪] - out, from

the album Fr - [♪] - ile was an example of this. This was [♪] new thing

for [♪] rock [♪] - nd to do and it was wi - [♪] - ly

[♪] - pt - [♪] by [♪] - ns and by

r- [♪] -io. Their most [♪] - mous album to [♪] -te is

Close to the [♪]. Many more chan - [♪] - s

o - [♪] - urr - [♪] and even An - [♪] - rson

l - [♪] - t. This h - [♪] [♪] [♪]

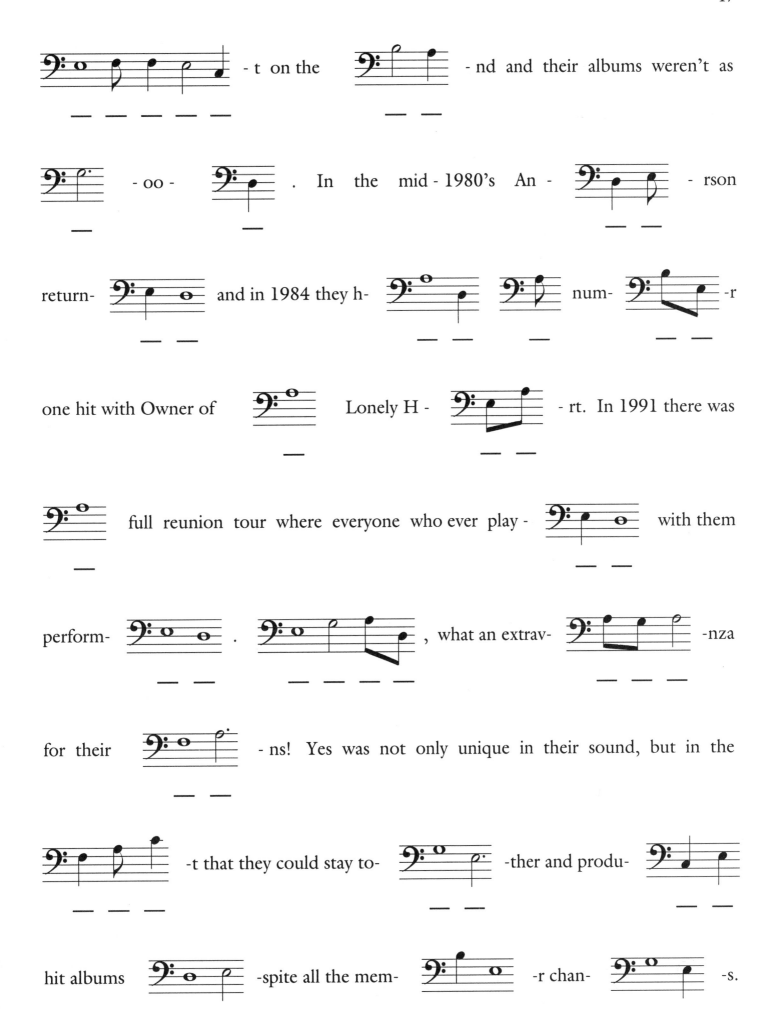

-t on the -nd and their albums weren't as -oo- . In the mid - 1980's An - rson return- and in 1984 they h- num- -r one hit with Owner of Lonely H - rt. In 1991 there was full reunion tour where everyone who ever play - with them perform- . , what an extrav- -nza for their -ns! Yes was not only unique in their sound, but in the -t that they could stay to- -ther and produ- hit albums -spite all the mem- -r chan- -s.

DOOBIE BROTHERS

Tom Johnston's first 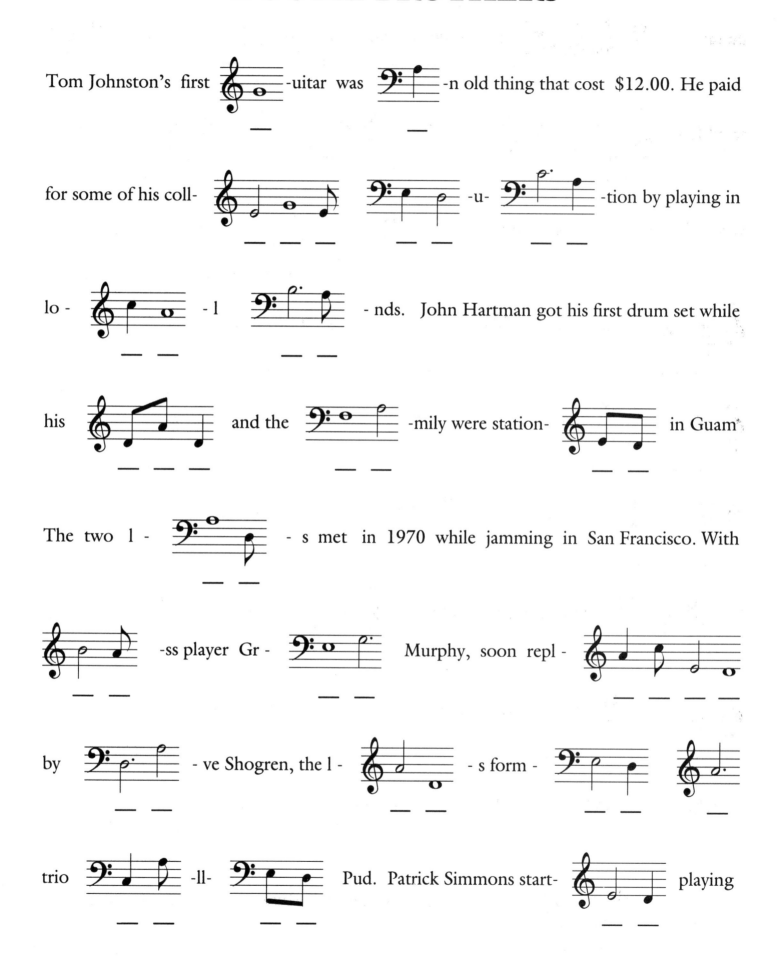 -uitar was -n old thing that cost $12.00. He paid

for some of his coll- -u- -tion by playing in

lo - -l - nds. John Hartman got his first drum set while

his and the -mily were station- in Guam

The two l - - s met in 1970 while jamming in San Francisco. With

-ss player Gr - Murphy, soon repl -

by - ve Shogren, the l - - s form -

trio -ll- Pud. Patrick Simmons start- playing

guitar at ♪♪♪ 8. While in coll - ♪♪♪ he ran ♪

small folk ♪♪♪♩○♪ and play- ♪♪♪ in lo- ♪○ -l clubs.

When the trio saw him sing and play they ♪♪♪♩·○ him to join the

♪♪♪ -nd. He ♪○ -r - ♪○♪ and the group

♪○♪♪ -me The Doobie Brothers. They got ♪○ r- ♪♪♪ -ord

♪○♩♪ -l almost imm - ♪♪♪ - iately with Warner Brothers. Over the

y- ♩·♪ -rs there were many mem- ♪♪♪ -r chan- ♪○ -s and

♪♩· s- ♪○♪ -ond drummer/percussionist was ♪♪♪♪♩·

to help their sound live. Their albums were gr- ♪♪♪ -tly su- ♪♪♪♪ -ssful

and boast - ♪♪♪ hits such as Listen to the Music, Long Train Running and

20

China Grove. In 1974 J - "Skunk" - xter play- on one of their r - ords. When his - nd, the well known St- -ly -n stopp- playing live he join - The Doobies full time. When Johnston - ll ill in 1975 another ex - St - -ly - n mem - - r, Mich - -l M - - onald's also gr- the -nd's roster. His presen- yet another dimension to the -nd's material and further incr - - s - their - me. Some hits they h - with him inclu - Takin' It To The

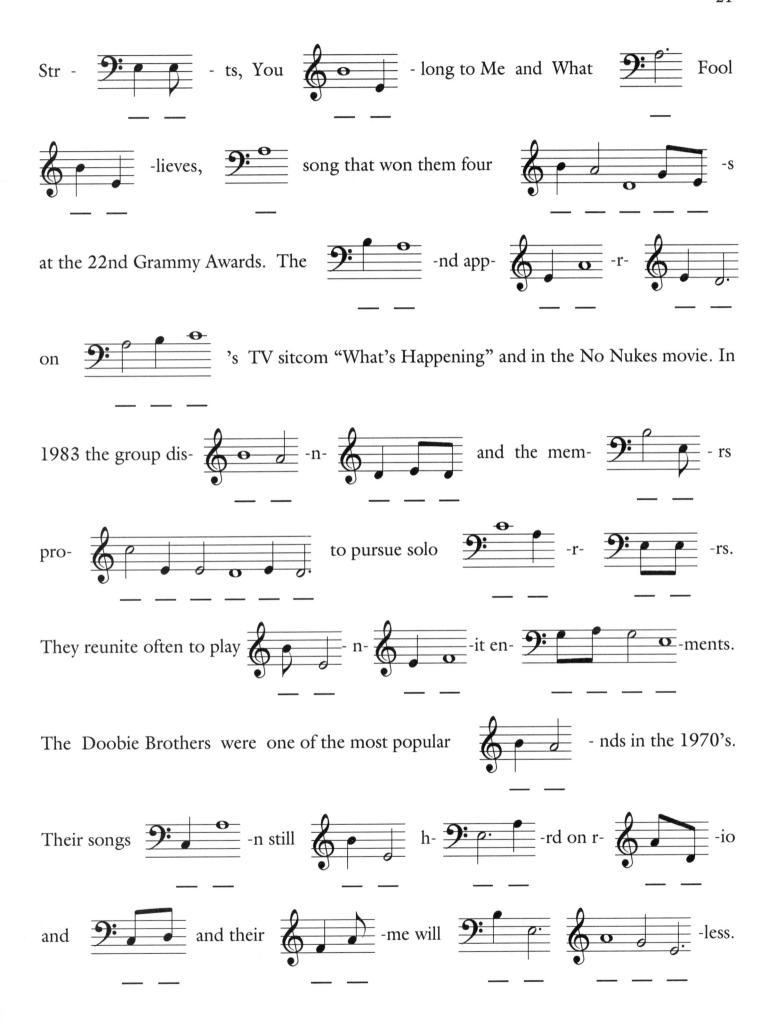

Str - ts, You - long to Me and What Fool

-lieves, song that won them four -s

at the 22nd Grammy Awards. The -nd app- -r-

on 's TV sitcom "What's Happening" and in the No Nukes movie. In

1983 the group dis- -n- and the mem- - rs

pro- to pursue solo -r- -rs.

They reunite often to play - n- -it en- -ments.

The Doobie Brothers were one of the most popular - nds in the 1970's.

Their songs -n still h- -rd on r- -io

and and their -me will -less.

21

QUEEN

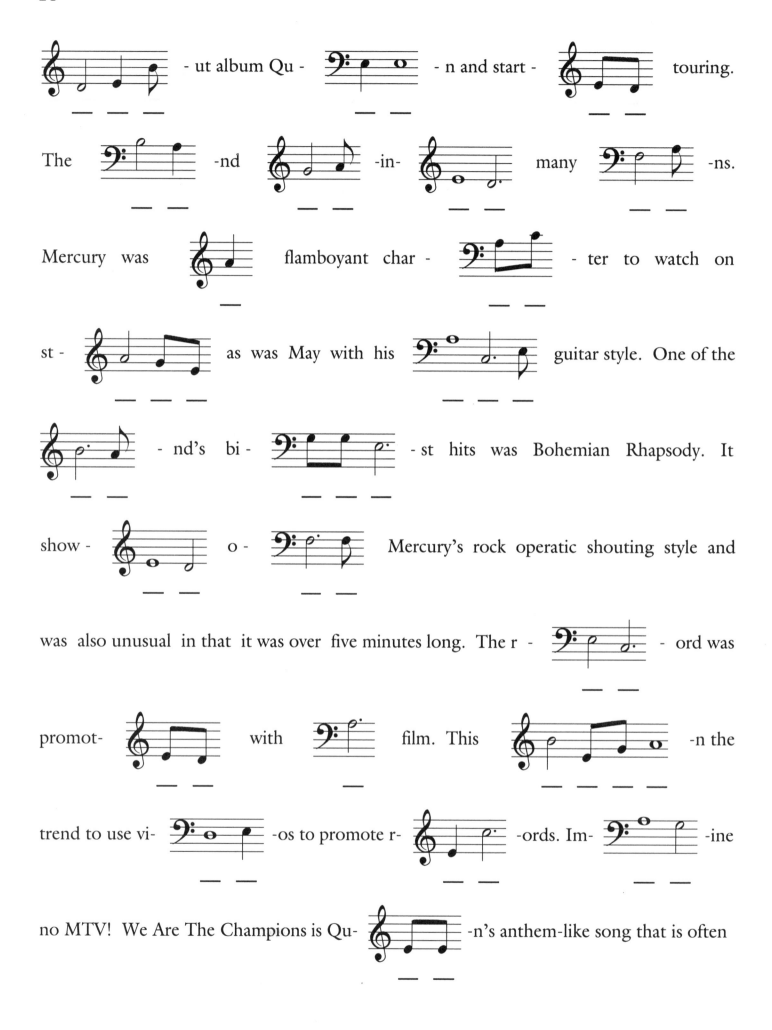

- ut album Qu - - n and start - touring.

The - nd - in- many -ns.

Mercury was flamboyant char - - ter to watch on

st - as was May with his guitar style. One of the

- nd's bi - - st hits was Bohemian Rhapsody. It

show - o - Mercury's rock operatic shouting style and

was also unusual in that it was over five minutes long. The r - - ord was

promot- with film. This -n the

trend to use vi- -os to promote r- -ords. Im- -ine

no MTV! We Are The Champions is Qu- -n's anthem-like song that is often play - 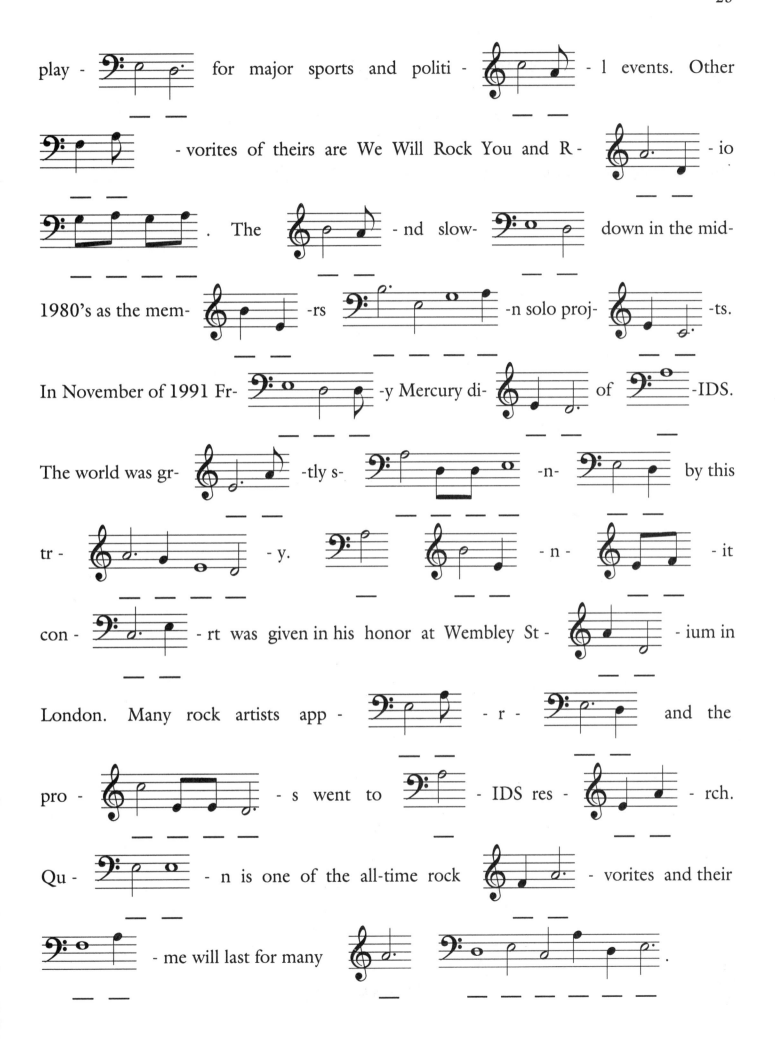 for major sports and politi - l events. Other

- vorites of theirs are We Will Rock You and R - io

. The - nd slow- down in the mid-

1980's as the mem- -rs -n solo proj- -ts.

In November of 1991 Fr- -y Mercury di- of -IDS.

The world was gr- -tly s- -n- by this

tr - - y. - n - - it

con - - rt was given in his honor at Wembley St - - ium in

London. Many rock artists app - - r - and the

pro - - s went to - IDS res - - rch.

Qu - - n is one of the all-time rock - vorites and their

- me will last for many .

MÖTLEY CRÜE

As ♪ -r ♪ -k as he could remem - ♪ -r,

Frank ♪ -rrano want - ♪ to ♪ ♪ musician.

He was ♪ ♪ s- ♪ and stole his first guitar. He

play- ♪ in ♪ group ♪ -ll- ♪ London

but left them in 1980 in s- ♪ -rch of his dr - ♪ -m

♪ - nd. Frank, now ♪ - lling himself Nikki Sixx,

want - ♪ ♪ ♪ -nd that ♪

looks, sound, songs and play - ♪ "shock rock". The first

mem - [music] - r he [music] was drummer Tommy

[music] - ss who later chan - [music] his name to Tommy

L- [music] . They found guitarist [music] - o - [music] [music] - l

from an [music] in [music] music paper. He [music] - me

known as Mick Mars. The thr- [music] l- [music] - s dy- [music]

their hair with the same blue - bl - [music] - k dye and [music] - me

Motley Crue. [music] - ing l - [music] sin - [music] - r

Vincent Neil Wharton, they claim - [music] to [music] the grossest

[music] -nd in the history of rock 'n' roll, willing to do anything to [music] -t

28

attention. At first these  boys of rock were rej- -t-

by every r - - ord company. R- - using to

-t- they put to - - ther their

first single and album on their own l - - l. They

pro- to throw copies into the audien - at

their shows. This unusual type of distribution l - to sold out shows and

eventually r - - ord - l. They

rel - - s - Shout At the - vil in 1983 and

29

-n world-wi- tour. The album was big su- -ss. -irls, Girls, Girls, was another big hit. In 1989 -ter many mishaps and tr- -ies, the -nd emer- with di- -rent im- . They put asi- their -st -nd in the world im- and releas- the album Dr. -lgood, major su- -ss. The -nd is number one with h- -vy metal -ns and has r- -iv- many -ol- -s and awards.

Rock Scrambler

Byrds
Crosby
Doobie Brothers
Freddy Mercury
Gene Clark
Genesis
Jon Anderson
Michael McDonald
Mick Mars
Motley Crue
Nash
Nikki Sixx
Peter Gabriel
Phil Collins
Queen
~~Roger McGuinn~~
Stills
Tommy Lee
Tony Banks
Yes
Young

Fill in the puzzle with each band or band member from the list. Roger McGuinn is provided to help you get started. Then unscramble the circled letters to discover an instrument that is played in all these bands.

— — — — — —

Rock Word Search

Brian May
Byrds
Chris Hillman
Chris Squire
Crosby
Dave Shogren
Doobie Brothers
Freddy Mercury
Gene Clark
Genesis
Jeff Baxter
John Deacon
Jon Anderson
Michael Clark
Michael McDonald
Mick Mars
Motley Crue
Nash
Nikki Sixx
Peter Gabriel
Phil Collins
Queen
Rick Wakeman
Roger McGuinn
Roger Taylor
Stills
Tommy Lee
Tony Banks
Yes
Young

D	M	S	G	E	N	E	C	L	A	R	K	Q	P	Z	L	T	U	C	N
A	O	B	K	Y	R	U	C	R	E	M	Y	D	D	E	R	F	C	I	X
U	T	O	B	N	D	A	V	E	S	H	O	G	R	E	N	M	K	A	E
I	L	O	B	F	A	J	Z	V	W	P	U	Q	S	A	C	K	Y	T	L
B	E	W	F	I	U	B	C	O	E	U	N	T	G	A	I	N	P	T	S
A	Y	R	R	B	E	C	Y	D	F	H	G	E	I	S	J	A	R	L	D
M	C	N	I	E	P	B	R	N	T	V	N	A	I	X	U	M	O	E	L
U	R	X	T	U	T	M	R	Z	O	E	U	X	E	I	S	L	G	I	A
S	U	H	M	N	Q	X	E	O	S	T	X	S	H	A	R	L	E	R	N
N	E	D	F	U	M	S	A	I	T	V	Y	A	M	N	A	I	R	B	O
I	J	S	T	I	L	L	S	B	V	H	Q	B	D	O	M	H	T	A	D
L	O	C	F	M	T	Z	L	I	F	U	E	G	G	S	K	S	A	G	C
L	H	U	X	T	N	V	S	D	R	F	T	R	U	R	C	I	Y	R	M
O	N	D	L	T	A	U	E	X	B	H	E	T	S	E	I	R	L	E	L
C	D	C	R	O	S	B	Y	I	O	Z	C	J	T	D	M	H	O	T	E
L	E	M	I	C	H	A	E	L	C	L	A	R	K	N	D	C	R	E	A
I	A	T	O	M	M	Y	L	E	E	P	X	C	D	A	E	U	M	P	H
H	C	B	X	R	O	G	E	R	M	C	G	U	I	N	N	E	S	C	C
P	O	U	N	A	M	E	K	A	W	K	C	I	R	O	D	T	U	E	I
L	N	T	V	P	C	U	B	Y	R	D	S	M	O	J	N	L	E	Q	M

The list above contains **30** bands or band members that you have just read about. Can you find all of them in the diagram? They can be read up, down, backwards, across or diagonally.

Rock 'n' Roll Misfits Game

In each group of four answers one does not fit in with the other three for reasons suggested in the clue above them. First complete the answers by writing the names of the notes in the spaces provided, then circle the misfit in each group.

1. Which one of these musicians was not a member of the band The Byrds?

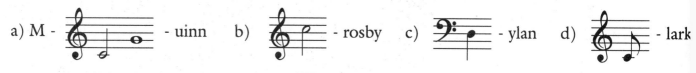

   a) M - 🎼 - uinn   b) 🎼 - rosby   c) 🎼 - ylan   d) 🎼 - lark

2. Which one of these songs was not a Queen hit?

   a) 🎼 - ohemian Rhapsody   b) We Will Ro - 🎼 - k You

   c) We 🎼 - re The 🎼 - hampions   d) Stairway To H - 🎼 - ven

3. Which one of these musicians was not in a band with the others?

   a) N - 🎼 - sh   b) 🎼 - rosby   c) 🎼 -ollins   d) Youn - 🎼

4. Which one of these was not a Doobie Brothers hit?

   a) T - 🎼 - kin' It To The Str - 🎼 - ts   b) Woo - 🎼 - stock

   c) You 🎼 - long To Me   d) What 🎼 Fool 🎼 - lieves

5. Which band had many member changes?

   a) Y - 🎼 - s   b) The 🎼 - yrds   c) Qu - 🎼 - n

   d) 🎼 - rosby, Stills, N - 🎼 - sh and Youn - 🎼

6. Which does not apply to Phil Collins?

   a) 🎼 - rummer   b) 🎼 - nesis member

   c) l - 🎼 singer   d) Wrote Woo - 🎼 - stock